On Blindness

Glyn Cannon

Methuen Drama

Published by Methuen 2004

1 3 5 7 9 10 8 6 4 2

First published in 2004 by
Methuen Publishing Limited
215 Vauxhall Bridge Road
London SW1V 1EJ

Methuen Publishing Limited Reg. No. 3543167

A CIP catalogue record for this book is available from the British Library

ISBN 0 413 77430 9

Typeset by Country Setting, Kingsdown, Kent

On Blindness

With thanks to Adam English, Kirin Saeed
and Rebecca Swift, and the Peggy Ramsay Foundation,
and to friends, family and Genny
for their love and rock-solid support

And with much love and many thanks
to Vicky, John, Lucy, Jenny, Steven and Scott
for their invaluable help in the writing of this play

For Lucy M and Gemma S

Characters

Edward, *thirty-two*
Shona, *twenty-nine*
Maria, *twenty-seven*
Greg, *seventeen*
Gaetano, *fifties or older*
Dan, *thirty-one*

Scene Two takes place simultaneously and continuously in two spaces that completely overlap each other on the stage.

The first, a room in Maria's house, is completely surrounded and enveloped by the second, Gaetano's studio (indicated by a vertical line to the left of the corresponding text). This means that the characters in the studio cross into and use the space of Maria's house, and may even also make use of the furniture in it, but the characters in each scene have no awareness of the other, and do not react to anything happening in the other scene. The director is encouraged to be as intricate and outlandish as she or he desires with the choreography, as long as neither split-scene acknowledges the existence of the other.

Scene One

Friday afternoon. A recording booth, small and restricted. Desk with computer, keyboard and microphone. And a man wearing headphones, who sips from a large mug of tea. **Edward** *is recording audio description between the dialogue he is listening to on the headphones, while watching a video image on the screen in front of him. He records it in a voice which is not flat, but is without too much inflection. He occasionally makes a mistake that requires him to backtrack and re-record his description.*

Edward Catherine and Nick are in her apartment, kissing on the bed; he is astride of Catherine, as she helps him to pull off his top.

He presses a key.

Catherine watches as Nick's kisses move down her body.

He presses a key.

She arches in pleasure as Nick's head goes down between her thighs –

He backtracks.

She arches in pleasure as Nick goes down –

He backtracks, and reconsiders the line.

She arches her body as Nick's head moves between her legs.

He presses a key.

With Catherine now on top of Nick, he looks up to see their reflection in a mirror on the ceiling. He watches as she kisses his stomach.

He stops. **Edward** *sips his tea. He stands, looks at his watch. He sits down again.*

Nick, um –

He backtracks.

Nick, now again on top of Catherine –

He backtracks.

Nick, again on top of Catherine –

He backtracks.

Nick, again on top of Catherine, enters her. They begin to move together.

He presses a key.

She pushes Nick, so that he rolls onto his back, with her astride him. She reaches behind his head to pull out a white scarf that she begins to tie Nick to the bedstead with. Nick looks apprehensive.

He presses a key.

As Catherine moves on top of Nick, she reaches behind herself, as though she is about to retrieve something. Then, as she –

He backtracks.

As Catherine moves on top of Nick, she reaches behind herself, as though she is about to retrieve something. Then, as she is, er –

He backtracks.

As Catherine moves on top of Nick, she reaches behind herself, as though she is about to retrieve something. Then, as she is climaxing, she suddenly collapses forward onto him.

He presses a key.

She rolls to lie beside him, and they kiss again.

He stops, and sips his tea. A red light flashes behind his head.
Shona *is at the door of the booth. He stands up and lets her in.*

Yes?

Shona (*looking at the screen*)   Ah . . . You'll go blind, Edward.

Edward   I am in the middle of something –

Shona *hands a mobile phone to him, mouthing 'Maria' and pointing at the phone.*

Oh, right, thanks. (*He takes the phone.*) Hello?

Shona   May I have a look?

Edward *and* **Shona** *swap places. She sits and puts on the headphones.*

Edward   Hi, yes, great, how are you? . . . No, of course, yes . . . Yes, I'm looking forward to it . . . I finish here about five and then I'll head straight down . . . Sure, let me just grab a, ah . . .

Shona *hands him a pad and pen from the desk.*

Edward   Thanks . . . Right, OK . . . yes . . . yes . . . I was thinking from . . . OK, right . . . bus stop, hut, yes . . . yes, another hut . . . red gate . . . cypress trees, OK, got it . . . OK, then . . . yes, see you then, yes . . . yes, bye. Bye.

Shona *turns to grin at* **Edward**.

Edward   What?

Shona   So . . . nervous?

Edward   Nervous? About what?

Shona   Your date.

Edward   Shona, that was a private telephone convers –

Shona   I'm sure it will go swimmingly.

Edward   Thank you.

Shona   Get her drunk and shag her. Can't go wrong.

Edward   Yes, thank you.

Shona   Don't rule it out.

Edward   I wasn't ruling anything out – I mean, there's nothing to rule out, Shona. I'm not looking for that, perhaps? I'm just going to meet a friend at her house, for dinner.

Shona   At her house?

Edward   Yes.

Shona   In the country?

Edward   Yes?

Shona   And you've not been there before?

Edward   No.

Shona   And you've just been out for coffee so far?

Edward   Well . . . we did go out to dinner the once, and a concert –

Shona   So you've been out a couple of times?

Edward   No, that was the same time, we went for dinner after –

Shona   And how did that resolve itself?

Edward   Resolve itself?

Shona   No goodnight kiss? Bit of a fumble? Bit of a feel of –

Edward   Look, ah, no, look, what do you think of this description? Since you are here.

Shona   Hmm . . . there's loads you've missed out.

Edward   Like what?

Shona   Like, she digs her nails into his back, he grabs her tits, that kind of thing.

Edward   I can't put everything in.

Shona   You have a bit more room than usual. There's no dialogue, is there?

Edward   Well, they are making . . . some noises.

Shona (*cutting over 'noises'*)   Oh, and this bit? She's not kissing his stomach.

Edward   What bit?

Shona   Here. 'With Catherine now on top of Nick, he looks up to see their reflection in a mirror on the ceiling. He watches as she kisses his stomach.' It's not his stomach she's kissing.

Edward   What?

Shona   Her head bobbing up and down? That's some very precise kissing going on.

Edward   I don't see –

Edward *looks at the video.*

Shona   She's giving him a blow job!

Edward   Oh. Well, you can't actually see she's doing that.

Shona   Edward, come on.

Edward   Oh, well . . . yes, it's suggested –

Shona   She's suggesting it pretty vigorously. And by that token: 'Nick's head moves between her legs.' He could be looking for a contact lens, for all we know.

Edward   OK, fair point.

Shona   And: 'He enters her.' All a bit religious, isn't it? The Holy Spirit came over her?

Edward   Yes, OK. Thank you.

Shona   You just need to be a bit sexier. You know the kind of thing.

Edward   Mmm.

Shona   Oh, and what's she about to 'retrieve'?

Edward   We're meant to think she's about to stab him. With an ice pick. Have you not seen this film?

Shona   No.

Edward   I thought it would be your kind of thing.

Shona   Oh no, too much sex in it for my liking. How did you meet her?

Edward   Meet? Maria? She came in and did those visual awareness sessions with us a few weeks back, remember?

Shona   I wasn't here for those. Who asked who out?

Edward   It wasn't like that. We'd just both fancied going to this concert, independent of each other –

Shona   Who mentioned it first?

Edward   Well, me. I said I had thought about going to this particular concert –

Shona   Who suggested going together?

Edward   No, it was mutual. Well, I *was* going to suggest it as well –

Shona   A-ha!

Edward   'A-ha' what?

Shona   She asked you out.

Edward   No, that's not what I said –

Shona   And now she's invited you over for dinner.

Edward   Yes, but, as a, um –

Shona   Hot date.

Edward   No.

Shona   Hot. Date. Hot. Date.

Edward   Shona, please, it is not a date.

Shona   Maria and Edward getting it *on* . . .

Edward   No. Look, I don't know why we're even discussing this. My plans for this evening are none of your business. It's not as if I constantly ask you –

Shona   Dan and I are having dinner with Gaetano.

Edward   Right.

Shona   He's a great cook it turns out. Being Italian. Sort of.

Edward   Gaetano, oh yes . . .

Shona   And Dan's not met him before. So that will be . . . interesting.

Edward   Great.

Beat.

Shona   So you're letting her do all the running?

Edward   Shona.

Shona   I'd had you down as quite a traditional *fellow*.

Edward   (*nothing*)

Shona   Guy asks three times before girl accepts? Man always pays? No holding hands until the third date?

Edward   (*nothing*)

Shona   Sorry. You know I only wind you up because it's Friday. And because I like you.

Edward   And . . .

Shona   And because it's easy.

Edward   . . . because it's easy. Yes. Great. Look, Shona, if that's the interrogation over, I really *do* have to get on.

Shona   And I'm a bit jealous.

Beat.

Edward   Jealous?

Shona   I miss it all.

Edward   Miss what?

Shona   The whole, y'know, meet somebody, call somebody, will they call you, the awkwardness, the newness . . . all that sort of thing.

Edward   I thought you just let them get you drunk and shag you?

Shona   That too. And the first kiss. It's funny – when you've had your lips around all sorts of appendages and your tongue in all sorts of orifices – but when they touch for that first *real* kiss, it's like they'd never touched before. And you know you're in for the long haul and the rough ride.

Edward   How romantic.

Shona   I think so. They should let me write one of these (*ie, the film*). What's she like?

Edward   Maria?

Shona   Maria.

Edward   Oh. She's . . . great. Very funny. Very clever, sharp. And very pretty.

Shona   And just a friend? Do you want to know how I judge it?

Edward   No.

Shona   I picture it, like a scene from a film, or a photograph, me and the prospective other, close my eyes and imagine it – and then . . . are we holding hands or not?

Edward   Oh, come on. Please.

Shona   No, really.

Edward   Shona, it's not funny, it isn't really a date –

Shona   No, seriously. Take me and Dan.

Edward   Mmm.

Shona   I hadn't seen him for a very long time. Years. And we hadn't even really been friends when we did know each other. Before. And then I bumped into him at a party. And we clicked. *Really* clicked. But you want to know you're not wasting your time and . . . well, I wasn't sure straight away. And then I closed my eyes. And there I was. And there was Dan. And we were . . . well, put it this way, it was a bit more than holding hands.

Edward   You surprise me.

Shona   (*not hearing him*)   But, you know, because I could see it . . . that gave me comfort that it was . . . worth pursuing. Worth taking a chance on.

Beat.

And then I knew it was love when I let him take me up the arse on our first date.

Edward *has nothing to say to this.*

Have fun.

She leaves **Edward** *to get back to work.*

Scene Two

Initially the stage is in darkness. Friday evening. A living room. A burgundy couch, a cream-white chair, an empty table. Growing shadows lengthening across the floor.

Maria So . . . there I am. It's a lovely day; there's warm sun on my face, and a breeze blowing down through the trees. Walking along the path, I'm aware of this man in front of me. I'm catching up with him. He's weighed down by this large . . . box of something. A bit too big for him, a bit awkward.

Greg Mmm.

Maria He takes a couple of steps, then he puts it down, very carefully. Takes his breath, as though he's just readjusting his grip – if you asked him. 'It's not too heavy for me,' he'd say, that's what he'd say he was doing.

Greg Yeah.

Maria But anyway, he gets his grip, takes another few steps, a couple less this time, puts it down carefully again . . . (*Laughs.*) He's fighting a losing battle here.

Greg Ah.

Maria But one more time, he tries. Finds his grip, lifts up the box, another couple of steps. But he loses it – it hits the path with a crunch and whatever's inside the box, it shatters into a hundred pieces. (*Laughs.*) Like crockery or something. (*Laughs.*)

Greg　Mmm.

Maria　I shouldn't laugh. It's not fair, really.

Greg　Mmm.

Maria　But . . . he hears me laugh. And he turns around.

Greg　Yeah.

Maria　And he takes a step towards me, he's angry. I can feel the steam coming off him, he's furious.

Greg　Mmm. Yeah.

A woman is sat on the sofa. And a young man is standing masturbating in front of her.

Maria　But then . . . (*Sighs.*) He sees me, he mumbles some apology . . . and I wish he would get angry. Just once.

Edward (*off*)　Hello? The front door is wide open?

Enter **Edward**. **Greg** *stops. Beat.*

Maria　Who's that?

Edward (*to* **Greg**)　What the hell are you doing?

Maria　Edward.

Edward　Get out.

Greg *makes no move.*

Edward　Go on! Get out! Piss off out of here!

Edward *chases* **Greg** *out, shouting. He comes back in.*

Maria　Edward? Is that you?

Edward　Yes, I'm here.

Maria　Edward, I wasn't expecting you this early –

Edward　There was . . . there was a boy in here.

Beat.

Maria　Er, yes . . . what happened? Why did you shout at him?

Edward Do you know him?

Maria What was he doing Edward? What did you see?

Edward You know him?

Maria Yes.

Edward Who is he?

Maria Greg.

Edward Greg?

Maria Yes.

Edward But who is he?

Maria The son of one of my neighbours.

Edward You're sure it was him?

Maria Yes.

Edward You're sure?

Maria Of course, I am. That was him.

Beat.

What did you see him – What was he doing?

Edward What was he doing?

Maria Yes.

Edward Mmm.

Maria What was he doing when you came in? You were shouting at him – where's he gone?

Edward He's, ah, I chased him out through the back. He's run off.

Beat.

Maria Why did you chase him out? Edward? What did you see him doing?

Edward He was . . . um . . .

Maria   What?

Edward   He was going through your things. I think he was looking for . . . something to steal.

Maria   He was . . . something to steal?

Edward   Yes.

Maria   Right. OK. Oh my God.

Edward   Mm.

Maria   Oh my God, he's round here all the time, he's never done . . . He's never been a problem before.

Edward   Well, young kids, teenagers . . . you know.

Maria   I can't believe he'd do that. Are you sure that that was what he was doing?

Edward   That's what I saw. That's what it looked like.

Maria   That's what it looked like?

Edward   Yes.

Rest.

Maria   Right. Should we . . . call the police?

Edward   No. I don't know, maybe. We don't need to do it just yet.

Maria   What did he steal?

Edward   He didn't get anything.

Maria   You're sure?

Edward   No.

Maria   He didn't have anything in his hands?

Beat.

Edward   Er, no. We don't need to call the police yet. I'll do it later.

Maria   No, it's OK. I can call them tomorrow myself.

Edward   I don't mind –

Maria   I'll call them myself. In a minute, maybe. Sit down.

Edward *sits.*

Maria   Are you OK?

Edward   I think so. He could have been . . . Anybody could have been in here.

Maria   Mmm. He's gone now, hasn't he? Would you like a drink? Calm you down?

Edward   Er, no, I'm – Are *you* OK?

Maria   I'm fine.

Edward   You're sure you're OK?

Maria   I'm fine, really.

Edward   Really? My heart is pounding.

Maria   Well – I'm jumping off the walls on the inside.

Beat.

Wow, I thought I could trust Greg. He always seemed a very honest young man.

Edward   Yes? Well, er, you can never be entirely certain about people, can you?

Maria   No, I guess not. He ran away pretty sharpish.

Edward   Yes.

Maria   You scared him off. Hadn't thought of you being quite that . . . masterful, Edward.

Edward   Er, yeah. Didn't know I had it in me.

Maria   Well, I suspected . . .

Rest.

You've had quite a bit of a shock. Walking in on that.

Edward   Er, yes. The front door was wide open.

Maria   Wide open?

Edward   Yes, I thought . . . well, anything . . .

Maria   He must have left it open when he came in. Or I left it open. Maybe I did when I let him in. He comes around a lot.

Edward   He does?

Maria   He fixes things for me.

Edward   Right. What was he fixing today?

Maria   Nothing today. Just came in for a chat.

Edward   Right.

Rest.

Maria   Not exactly the welcome I was anticipating. Sorry.

Edward   It's hardly your fault.

Beat.

Maria   I'm . . . so surprised at Greg. I thought I could trust him.

Edward   Er. Yes. I'm sorry.

Beat.

Maria   But as you said, he hasn't taken anything.

Edward   Absolutely. Sorry. Yes. Well, as far as I can tell. Sorry.

Maria   What are you sorry for, Edward?

Edward   Sorry, you're right, no – er, sorry. Er, no. Nothing.

Rest.

Wow.

Maria   Mm.

Edward   What an exciting moment.

Maria   Yes.

Edward   Yes.

Maria   Well . . . After all that . . . welcome.

Edward   Thank you.

Maria   Do you like it?

Edward   It's a lovely house, yes. Bigger than I thought from what you've said.

Maria   Would you like the grand tour?

Edward   No, I'm fine.

Maria   It's not a problem.

Edward   No, really . . . I'm happy to sit here for a few moments. Get my breath back.

Edward *retrieves a lighter and a pack of cigarettes from his pockets.*

Maria   So my directions were OK then?

Edward   Perfect. Made good time.

Maria   Very good time.

Edward   Well, the taxi driver seemed to know where he was going. Said he knew who you were.

Maria   They all do there – you came by train then?

Edward   Yes.

Maria   I thought you were driving out.

Edward   Oh no, I can't drive. Kept failing my test, terrible driver.

Maria   Really? Me too. That explains it then.

Edward   What?

Maria   You were a bit earlier than I expected.

Edward   Right.

Beat.

Maria   A good thing you were. By the sounds of it.

Edward   Yes. Probably was.

Edward *lights up.*

Maria   You weren't a smoker last Tuesday?

Beat.

Edward   Oh. No, I'm not one really, I had given up . . . a bit – sorry –

Maria   It's not a problem.

Edward   – not thinking, I'll smoke outside.

He gets up.

Maria   No, it's fine.

Edward   Sorry, it's a terrible habit.

He looks for somewhere to stub it out, finding nowhere, settles awkwardly for the sole of his shoe, and puts the cigarette back in the packet.

First packet I've bought for a couple of weeks though. Progress of a sort. It's a nervousness thing.

Maria   It's not a problem. There is an ashtray somewhere –

Edward   I can wait.

Maria   I really don't mind. Are you feeling nervous then?

Edward   Nervous? Oh, no . . .

Maria   What are you feeling nervous about, Edward?

Edward   Ah . . .

> — *And here is where it begins to get complicated.* —

> *An artist's studio. A chair. A couch. Easels, tables, canvas, floorboards. Every inch spattered with paint. The lights come up in* **Gaetano**'s *studio: this overlaps and envelopes the first space. The furniture in the centre of the studio is coincidentally the same as that in Maria's front room . . . Enter* **Shona**. *She is wearing an unzipped dress that she has just put on, and carrying a mobile phone.*

Shona (*to off*) You don't have any mirrors in here.

Maria I'm only teasing, Edward. Edward?

Edward Ah, actually, maybe I should have that drink?

Maria OK . . .

Gaetano *comes in, drying his hands on a small towel.*

Gaetano No, you're absolutely right, I don't.

Maria Whisky?

Edward (*simultaneously*) Cup of tea?

Gaetano (*simultaneously*) Glass of wine?

Maria OK, compromise – how about a glass of wine?

Edward Er, yes, wine would be fine, thank you.

Gaetano Do you really need one (*ie, a mirror*)? You look great.

Shona No, I'll live. Yes, please.

Maria *stands to go out.*

Maria White or red?

Gaetano Mm?

Shona Glass of wine.

Gaetano Oh, right yes. *He moves to leave.*

Shona Hang on –

Maria Edward?

Shona – can you zip me up please?

Gaetano Yes, of course.

He does so. He goes out again. **Shona** *sets about looking for something.*

Maria Any preference? Edward?

| **Shona** (*to off*)   Gaetano?

Edward   Er, yes, wine, I was just thinking.

Maria   Yes, I could hear the cogs turning.

Edward   What if he comes back?

Maria   Greg? So what if he does?

| **Shona**   Did you see where I put my watch?

Maria   I mean – why would he come back? You chased him off didn't you?

Edward   Yes, but –

Maria   Why would he come back, then? To the scene of the crime?

Beat.

Edward   No, probably not, no.

Maria *sits.*

Maria   He's just a kid, don't worry about it. I'm sure he won't come back. He's a good person . . . generally.

Edward   Well, yes, but –

Maria   Perhaps you could do the honours, wine's in the fridge, bottle-opener in the drawer, could you put it back in the same place, please?

Edward   Oh yes, of course.

Edward *goes to retrieve the wine.*

> **Gaetano** *comes back in carrying a bottle of champagne, an opener, two glasses and a small ice-bucket. He sets about opening the bottle.*
>
> **Gaetano**   Out of wine – champagne?
>
> **Shona**   Oh, yes please. Having another look at it, were we?
>
> **Gaetano**   A final glance, maybe.

Shona Not much you can do about it now.

Gaetano No. Well, you have to . . . y'know, draw a line . . .

Shona Ha. Draw a line.

Gaetano Oh yes, I see. Draw a line, yes

Shona I didn't see you do much this afternoon.

Gaetano You can't see what I'm doing, can you?

Shona That's true. You could be doing anything behind there. I was thinking . . . bet this couch has got some stories.

Gaetano Some.

Gaetano *pours* **Shona** *a glass of champagne.*

Shona I bet you've had plenty of women on this.

Gaetano Maybe.

Shona Who? Anyone famous?

Gaetano Famous. Mmm.

Shona Who? Who was the last one?

Gaetano Oh . . . it was a while ago.

Shona What was she like?

Gaetano The last one?

Shona Yes.

Gaetano Before you?

Shona Yes.

Gaetano She was . . . She had very pale skin, and very big, green eyes. Freckles on her shoulders. Just her shoulders.

Shona Freckles? Lovely.

Gaetano I thought so.

Rest.

Shona   What time is it? Where is that watch?

Gaetano   You must have left it in the − I'll get it, hang on.

He goes to retrieve her watch. **Shona** *sits on the couch.*

Edward *comes back in with a couple of glasses of wine.*

Maria   That was quick. Thank you.

She drinks it in fairly large swigs. **Edward** *sips. Awkward moment.*

Shona's *mobile rings. She looks for it to answer it.*

Shona (*on phone*)   Hello?

Edward   Lovely kitchen.

Maria   Thank you.

Shona   Yes?

Maria   Are you hungry?

Shona   Where are you?

Edward   Ah . . . Not sure.

Maria   No? I was going to make something, nothing amazingly exciting . . . but . . .

Shona   OK, well, keep walking then . . . No, you can't miss it . . . Yes, next door along, yes . . . Ring when you're outside, OK? Yeah, bye . . .

Rest.

Edward   Ah . . . Are you sure you're OK?

Maria   Yes. Why shouldn't I be?

Edward   It was . . . It must have been −

Maria   I'm fine, Edward. Really. He was just messing around. Probably. It's not that big a deal.

Beat.

I've forgotten about it now. I've calmed down.

Edward   If you're sure –

Maria   I'm absolutely sure.

Beat.

Edward   OK . . . But, look, if –

Maria   All right, you can make me some sugary tea and run me a warm bath if it'd make you any happier. I'm fine, *really*.

Edward   Oh, well, sure if you want. Whatever helps.

Beat.

Maria   What?

Edward   If you want to have a bath – yeah do, go ahead.

Maria   Have a bath?

Beat.

Edward   Yeah. If you . . . want one.

Maria   Well . . . if you think that might be . . . a good idea.

Edward   Yeah. Sure.

Beat.

Maria   Right.

She stands.

I'll go run that bath then.

Edward   Great, no problem whatsoever. I'll just . . . um . . .

Maria   Make yourself comfortable.

Edward   Make myself comfortable. Yes.

Maria   Great. I'll be . . . in the bath . . .

Edward   Right.

She leaves.

OK. Great.

> **Gaetano** *returns with* **Shona***'s watch, as well as her earrings in his pocket, and a small pile of books, small portfolios, albums and the like. He hands* **Shona** *the watch, and then sets about setting up an easel / stand.*
>
> **Shona**   Thank you.
>
> **Gaetano**   You forgot these as well (*the earrings*).
>
> **Shona**   Sorry he's late.
>
> **Gaetano**   That's not a problem.
>
> **Shona**   I did draw him a map.

Edward   Great.

Edward *is distinctly uncomfortable.*

> **Shona**   I didn't even realise I'd taken these off. Not really dressed without them.
>
> **Gaetano**   Nor naked with them.
>
> *Beat.*
>
> **Shona**   Er, yeah. What are those (*the books*)?
>
> **Gaetano**   Oh yes, I finally remembered to bring these. My . . . body of work.
>
> **Shona**   Ah! At last!
>
> **Shona** *grabs the book on the top of the pile and flicks through, absorbed in each picture.*
>
> These are great.
>
> **Gaetano**   Thank you. Nice to finally show you I can paint a bit.
>
> **Shona**   I'd have found out eventually.
>
> **Gaetano**   I'm . . . bemused. I would have looked me up. If it was me.

Shona   Meant to. Never got around to it.

Gaetano   Very trusting of you, nonetheless.

Shona   Can't do suspicious. Don't have the eyebrows.

Edward *gets out a cigarette and a lighter and heads outside to smoke it.*

Wow, this one's beautiful. What about her? Did you have an affair with her?

Gaetano *looks.*

Gaetano   Oh God, no.

Shona   Why? What's wrong with her?

Gaetano   What was right with her? She was a royal pain in the arse.

Shona   Yeah?

Gaetano   A couple of months pregnant and didn't tell me before sitting. I was beginning to wonder why I was running out of paint so quickly.

Shona   I doubt she got pregnant just to piss you off. Was it −?

Gaetano   No.

Beat.

Shona   Well . . . these are really good. You're a great painter.

Gaetano   Thank you.

Shona   I shall look properly at them after dinner. How am I looking?

Gaetano   Very pretty. He's very lucky.

Shona   It's not for him, necessarily.

Beat.

Maybe I just dressed up for *myself*.

Beat.

Gaetano   Well . . . He'll be knocked sideways nonetheless.

Shona   Better had be. I'm moving in with him. His new place.

Edward *comes back in.*

Edward (*calling up*)   Maria? Maria, I'm just going, er, nipping outside for . . . a, um . . .

He goes out again.

Gaetano   You are?

Shona   Yes.

Gaetano   When are you doing that, then?

Shona   Next weekend.

Gaetano   Uh-huh.

Shona   And he wants to sign half the flat over to me. What do you think?

Gaetano   That's a bit flash.

Shona   Really?

Gaetano   I don't know. What do you think?

Beat.

Shona   If you're not going be helpful . . .

Gaetano   Well, great. It sounds great.

Shona   We'll see how it goes first.

Gaetano   This isn't a good thing?

Beat.

Shona   Yes, it is.

Gaetano   OK. Congratulations. Cause for celebration, then. Maybe I should nip out and get us another bottle.

Shona   Easy, it's not as if we're getting *married* . . .

He returns to setting up the easel, bringing in a large canvas, covered.

So . . . this last woman on the couch before me. Did you fuck her as well?

Gaetano   As well?

Beat.

Shona   As well as painting her?

The mobile rings. **Shona** *picks it up.*

Hello? . . . Yeah, he'll be down. OK . . . It's Dan, he's outside.

Gaetano   OK. No peeking.

Gaetano *heads down to let* **Dan** *in.* **Shona** *pauses for a moment before lifting a corner of the sheet covering the canvas to sneak a look. She does not get much of a chance before she hears voices coming in and stands back.* **Dan** *and* **Gaetano** *come in.* **Dan** *looks a bit like a catalogue model, only shorter. He is wearing a suit and tie.*

Dan   Yeah, I didn't see it the first time I walked past.

Gaetano   It can be quite easy to miss.

Dan   Yeah. It, er, must cause problems.

Gaetano   Problems?

Dan   For . . . deliveries, and things like that . . .

Gaetano   Sometimes, I suppose.

Dan   It's pretty dark out there. (*To* **Shona**.) Hiya, gorgeous.

He kisses her hello.

Shona   Hi.

Dan   Sorry, I'm late. I was just saying –

Shona   Dark outside, yes.

Gaetano   Club should be open by now. That tends to light up the front of the building.

Dan   That club, that's a, er, a −

Gaetano   Strip bar? Yes, or tabletop dancing, whatever they call it.

Dan   Right. How does that work out, then?

Gaetano   Fine. Means I know my car is still going to be outside when I leave. Both hungry?

Dan   Always.

Shona   Famished.

Gaetano   Good, I'll get cooking. I've opened some booze, there, Dan. Help yourself.

Dan   Thanks.

He leaves.

Hello.

Shona   You're late.

Dan   Said sorry.

Shona (*being* **Dan**)   'That club that's a, er, a −'

Dan   What?

Shona   Don't you bankers have lap-dance radar or something? I said to look for the strippers.

Dan   Actually, I'm known in the office as the shy, sensitive, artistic one.

Shona   Sensitive bollocks.

Dan   Aching a little bit at the moment, maybe.

He kisses her hello properly.

Shona   Missed you.

Dan   Missed you too.

Shona   So, how was Switzerland?

Dan   Yeah, same as ever. Swiss.

Shona   And how was the flight?

Dan   A bit bumpy.

Shona   Were you scared?

Dan   Funny, I'm only scared when you're sat next to me.

Shona   Yeah?

Dan   Yeah, funny that, isn't it?

Shona   Hilarious. And what did you get me? Chocolate?

Dan (*with 'chocolate'*)   Chocolate.

Shona   Great.

Dan   There was the fattest woman ever in front of me at the airport this morning.

Shona   Really?

Dan   Really. I mean, like, in waves. Waves of fat. A big tidal wave of fat. The check-in staff looked terrified.

Shona   Did she manage to get on the plane?

Dan   Dunno. We managed to take off, so maybe not. (*Laughs.*) Yeah, I can see the security at the gate, trying to stop her with tranquiliser darts. 'Nooo! Stay away from the plane!' And her teeth! Fuck! I've never seen teeth like that. You know, just sticking out from under her lip like . . . big . . . teeth. I didn't think anyone could look like that. In this day and age.

Shona   What does it matter what she looks like? She was probably a very sweet, charming person.

Dan   I didn't say she wasn't.

Shona   No, true.

Dan   I wouldn't like to presume either way.

Shona   No, all right.

Rest.

Dan   He's older than I thought.

Beat. **Dan** *pours himself a glass of champagne*

Shona   How old did you think he was?

Dan   I don't know. Older than that. Guy, er –

Shona   Gaetano (*ie, Guy-tah-no*).

Dan   Gae –

Shona   – tano.

Dan   Him. Yeah. I thought he was a friend of yours.

Shona   He is a friend of mine.

Dan   You know what I mean.

Shona   What do you mean?

Dan   I thought he was a college friend of yours or something.

Shona   He isn't.

Dan   No, he seems very interesting.

Shona   He is.

Gaetano *pops his head back in.*

Gaetano   Dan, sorry, I forgot to ask: how are you with seafood?

Dan   Not bad, most people tend to prefer a little wedge of lemon though.

Beat.

Gaetano   Sorry?

Shona He'll eat anything in front of him, Gaetano.

Dan Absolutely.

Gaetano OK, good.

Dan I was saying to Shona, nice place you have here.

Gaetano Thank you. OK, almost ready.

Gaetano *goes back to the kitchen.*

Shona Have you been drinking?

Dan He's not gay, is he?

Shona No, I don't think so. Why?

Dan Just wondering. A lot of these older painter types are, though, aren't they? A bit . . . fruity?

Shona I wouldn't know.

Beat.

Dan He reminds me a bit of your dad.

Shona He's not at all like my dad.

Dan No, but . . . y'know what I mean.

Shona He is nothing like my dad. You're not going to be a prick this evening, are you, Dan?

Beat.

Dan Am I often one, then?

Shona No, you know I don't mean that.

Dan I'm sorry. I am trying not to be. Best behaviour. Scout's honour.

Shona I did help to entertain your pervy business friend.

Dan Associate.

Shona And he did stare at my chest all evening.

Dan   And it was very much appreciated – I mean you entertaining, not your –

Shona   Tits.

Dan   Tits, yes. It meant a lot to me.

Rest.

So. He's a painter?

Shona   Yes.

Dan   A famous painter?

Shona   Yes. I think he was, yes.

Dan   Would I have heard of him?

Shona   How many painters can you name?

Dan   No, fair enough. Have *you* heard of him?

Beat.

Shona   Yes.

Dan   And is this one of his, then?

Dan *goes to look under the sheet.*

Shona   No! You can't look yet.

Dan   Look at what? What is it? A painting of you?

Shona (*nothing*)

Dan   It *is* a painting of you?

Shona   A portrait, yes.

Dan   Really?

Dan *goes again to try and look under the sheet.*

Shona   Dan, no! After dinner. He's going to unveil it then.

Dan   Unveil it? What does it look like?

Shona   I don't know.

Dan   You don't know?

Shona No, Gaetano wouldn't let me look. Quite strict about that.

Dan You must have some idea.

Shona No. And I didn't ask. It's his painting.

Beat.

Dan So this is a painting of you under here?

Shona Yes.

Dan It's yours?

Shona No, I just posed for it.

Beat.

Dan So, it's not yours?

Shona That's right.

Dan What's it for?

Shona I don't know. To sell. Like any other painting.

Dan It's for sale?

Shona It might be, yes.

Beat.

Dan That would be great, to have a portrait of you. That would be great. Shall I buy it off him? How much do you think he'd sell it for?

Shona I don't know.

Dan *takes this all in.*

Dan That's quite impressive.

Shona Er, yes.

Dan Like an actual painter.

Shona He is an actual painter.

Dan That's very quick work.

Beat.

Shona   Quick work?

Dan   How long did it take?

Shona   I don't know. A month in total.

Dan   A month. Uh-huh.

Shona   If you take the actual time, but in real time, once or twice a week, since . . . January.

Dan   January? Each week? I thought . . . a day or two. When have you have been doing all that?

Shona   You know my yoga lessons?

Dan   Yes?

Shona   When I said I was at yoga lessons –
I wasn't, I was here.

Edward *comes back in, not much calmed down by his cigarette. Beat.*

Dan   You were here?

Shona   Yes.

Dan   Posing for this?

Shona   Yes.

Beat.

Dan   Oh . . . you were lying to me?

Shona   Well, only about where I was going. And that I know anything about yoga.

Dan   Only?

Shona   Think of it as an art class rather than a yoga class.

Dan (*nothing*)

Shona   Yeah. With only me and Gaetano in the class, of course . . .

Dan   And were you going to tell me about it?

Shona I don't know – I just didn't want to talk about it.

Dan Right. Why not?

Beat.

Edward *remembers something in his pocket he had forgotten about – a CD.*

Shona I just didn't want to talk to anybody about it.

Dan You didn't tell anybody about it?

Shona No. I think I mentioned it to Edward once, maybe, but . . .

Dan Edward? Who the hell's Edward?

Shona Edward at work.

Dan Oh. The . . . gay one?

Shona He's not gay. Either.

Dan You said he was.

Shona I said repressed, a bit uptight, maybe, chronically shy. That doesn't equal gay. Just like 'painter'.

Dan So you talked it through with Edward?

Shona No, I was just explaining why I was taking an afternoon off, probably. It's not a big fucking deal, Dan.

Rest.

Dan OK. Why did you fancy getting your portrait done?

Shona I hadn't been thinking about it. I mean, it wasn't my idea, was it?

Beat.

He asked me if I'd pose for it.

Dan   He just wandered up to you in the street and asked if you'd pose for a picture?

Shona   Pretty much, yes.

Dan   And you agreed?

Shona   Not at first, no.

Dan   But you changed your mind?

Shona   Well, yes.

Dan   And what made you do that?

Shona   I don't know. I just did.

Dan   You don't know?

Shona   Actually . . . Yes, I do know. That big space above the mantelpiece in your flat.

Dan   Big space?

Shona   Yes. I was sat there one Sunday –

Dan   In my flat? Where was I?

Shona   You were in the country. I don't know. Next to me. Watching the motor-racing or something. Or asleep probably. But there I was one Sunday, looking at the big space above your mantelpiece and I thought . . . I could see it there. I could see it above the mantelpiece in your flat.

Dan   So you *are* buying it?

Shona   No, I'm not, I could just see it going there.

Dan (*crestfallen*)   Oh.

Shona   What?

Dan   I've ordered a big mirror from the catalogue, I was going to put that there.

Shona   No, not *actually* there. I could just see it there. It . . . fitted the room. It suited the flat.

Dan   Uh-huh.

Shona Do you . . . see what I mean?

Dan *thinks.*

Edward *heads into the kitchen.*

Dan OK. Cool. Great.

Shona What?

Dan I think it's great.

Shona You do?

Dan Yes.

Shona If I'd talked to you about it, I wouldn't have gone through with it. Do you understand that?

Dan No, I think it's a great idea. Having a potrait of you. Fantastic.

Shona Good.

Beat.

Dan I wouldn't have been bothered, though.

Shona Yeah, but –

Dan I think it's a great idea. You're beautiful.

Shona Thank you, but –

Dan I wouldn't have said, 'No, you can't do it.'

Shona What?

Beat.

Dan I wouldn't have said, 'No, don't do it.'

Beat.

Shona I don't think I would have *asked*.

Gaetano *comes back in.*

Gaetano Almost ready. Everything OK?

Shona Great. Just have to, um . . . wash my hands.

She leaves.

Edward *comes back in, having refilled his glass, and has in his hand a flapjack, which he is eating. He stands around for a moment, sipping his wine.*

Awkward pause. The two men stand around for a moment, sipping their wine.

Dan   So . . . What's for dinner?

Gaetano   Tagliatelle.

Dan   Oh, yeah. Is it the fresh pasta they do? Shona and I love using that, rather than the dried stuff.

Gaetano   Actually . . . I was a pasta chef briefly when I was young. So I like to make it from scratch.

Dan   Oh. Right.

Gaetano   Do you cook much yourself, then? Aside from the pasta?

Dan   Oh yeah, like do a curry or something from scratch now or then.

Gaetano   Really? Thai, Indonesian, that kind of thing?

Dan   Yeah. That kind of thing. So . . . I gather we're having a grand unveiling this evening, then.

Gaetano   Yes. First time I've done this in years. Very exciting.

Dan   Oh right. How long has it been?

Gaetano   Oh . . . fifteen. Twenty years.

Dan   Twenty years?

Gaetano   This is me finally getting back to it. Shona's my first portrait since . . . a long time ago.

Dan   Right. Great. Make much from all this, then?

Gaetano Sold something here and there. But I've made money elsewhere as well.

Dan Right.

Beat.

So are you actually any good, then?

Gaetano I have my moments. I had my time in the sun, I suppose, but I was never going to be premier league material, no, but . . .

Dan (*nothing*)

Gaetano And I'm not very well-practised right now . . . Yes, not bad.

Beat.

Dan No, I mean it. Are you actually any good?

Gaetano (*nothing*)

Shona *returns.*

Shona Smells ready in there.

Gaetano Good. Yes. Yes, let's eat.

Dan Magic.

They go to eat.

Maria *comes back in, now wearing a towelling dressing-gown.* **Edward** *is still eating, and has a mouthful of flapjack.*

Maria Edward?

Edward Mmf. Yemf, I'mf herf.

Maria Ah, you found something to eat, then?

Edward Yempf. Er, yes.

Maria Good. I hope you don't think this is . . . slovenly. I didn't bother getting dressed again.

Edward No.

Maria   I've . . . 'slipped into something more comfortable'.

Edward   That certainly . . . looks comfortable, yes.

Maria   You think so?

Edward   I mean – my aunt's got one just like that. She says they're, um . . .

Beat.

Maria   So you did find something to eat? I'm sorry I've been so disorganised –

Edward   No, these are great, they'll do me fine. Are they locally made?

Maria   What are 'these'?

Edward   Sorry, flapjacks, sorry.

Maria   That's OK.

Edward   I'm sorry.

Maria   No, I'm sorry. Flapjacks not much of a proper meal. I was going to cook something a bit more . . . Well. Never mind.

Beat.

Edward   Ah, I forgot earlier. I brought you something.

Maria   I didn't need you to bring anything, Edward.

Edward *hands her the CD.*

Maria   What's on this?

Edward   It's a recording. Of the concert.

Maria   Oh. Thanks.

Beat.

Edward   Well, not exactly. My friend that got us the seats? The engineer. He did me another favour as well. They have an ambient mic that he mixed in for me.

Maria   Oh, right.

Edward   The snorer? He's there right in front of you.

Maria   Oh. And the seat-kicker?

Edward   All in glorious surround sound. It's a truly terrible live bootleg.

Maria   Oh, thank you very much. That's very . . . sweet.

Edward   It's an absolute pleasure. And I put some other bits and bobs I thought you might like on there.

Maria   Thank you.

She kisses him.

Edward   Ah, so how's work been?

Maria   Fine. Boring.

Edward   Me too. Same as ever.

Maria   How's Shona?

Edward   Same as ever.

Maria   Sounds like she winds you up.

Edward   She's a master at it.

Maria   That's a sign she likes you, isn't it?

Edward   Likes me?

Maria   You're her friend.

Edward   She's not particularly mine.

Maria   As far as she's concerned you are.

Edward   She's nosey.

Maria   She's interested in you.

Edward   She could be less interested. I don't really like . . . people knowing my business.

Maria   Maintain the mystery.

Edward   What?

Maria   You like to stay mysterious and intriguing, do you?

Edward   And do I?

Maria   You manage it quite well, yes.

Beat.

Edward   It's a lovely view outside.

Maria   Outside?

Edward   I nipped outside for a smoke –

Maria   You can smoke in here.

Edward   I wanted the fresh air. Calm down. After all that with –

Maria   Right.

Beat.

Edward   And it's a lovely view from your garden. Of the valley.

Maria   Er, yes. It is.

Edward   The sun setting, it sort of spills down the side of the hill onto those houses.

Beat.

They're quite new estates, aren't they? They look like giant toy bricks down there, snaking round the valley like –

Maria   Yes, I remember it.

Edward   Really?

Maria   Yes. This house belonged to my grandparents.

Edward   Oh, yes, I see. And they've left it entirely to you, that's right?

Maria   Yup. And pissed off a lot of my family in the process.

Edward   Wow. Completely to you?

Maria   Yes.

Edward   How long have you had it?

Maria   About . . . ten months now.

Edward   Oh, I'm sorry.

Maria   What for? I got given a house.

Edward   No, but you must have been quite close. To your grandparents.

Maria   Oh. Not really. I suppose so, no more than anybody else, though. Yes, it was sad, but they were getting on.

Edward   Oh . . . but . . . you remember the view?

Maria   Yes.

Edward   You were . . . fifteen? . . . When you lost it?

Beat.

Maria   Fifteen, yeah.

Edward   That's quite young.

Maria   Well, it hurt a bit at the time, but I was pretty glad to be shot of it.

Beat.

Sorry, we are talking about my virginity, aren't we?

Edward (*nothing*)

Maria   No, fuck, sorry, that was . . . forget I said that.

Rest.

Edward   So, uh, what did you miss most −?

Maria   Playing Scrabble. I could really do with another glass of wine, could you get me one please?

Edward   Er, yes. Sure. *He leaves.* **Maria** *gathers herself.* **Edward** *comes back in with a glass of wine which he hands to* **Maria**. *She drinks it quite quickly.*

Maria   Are you having one?

Edward   Oh.

Maria   Bring the bottle in, Edward.

Edward *goes to get himself one.* **Maria** *moves from the armchair to the sofa.* **Edward** *comes back in and sits in the armchair.*

Edward   There we go.

Maria   I just thought, I'm always worried about spilling wine on that chair.

Edward   Oh. OK.

Edward *gets up and sits next to* **Maria**. *Slightly awkward pause.*

Maria   I went to the cinema the other day.

Edward   Oh, really?

Maria   Not one of yours, I'm afraid.

Edward   Oh. Well, I'm sure my colleague . . . did his or her best. I try to pass on some of the genius.

Maria   Mmm. Well, this film my friend had chosen . . . it got a bit raunchy.

Edward   Raunchy?

Maria   Yes.

Edward We've had a few like that in recently.

Maria How do you deal with them?

Edward It's funny you should ask that –

Maria I'm sure you take it all in your stride.

Edward Er, yeah. It's all just part of the service. Listen to me, I sound like a fireman.

Maria Nothing wrong with firemen.

Edward Er, no, nothing at all . . .

Maria How do you do it?

Edward Oh, you know, just . . . say what you see.

Maria Can you give me any examples?

Edward Uh . . .

Maria Off the top of your head?

Edward Er . . .

Maria 'He leans over, brushes his hand softly over her face, then pulls her red lips towards his, roughly grabbing her by the . . .'?

Awkward moment, **Edward** *unable to find something to say.*

> **Dan** *comes in to retrieve the champagne.*
>
> **Dan** (*to off*) No, it's fine, there's still plenty of this left.
>
> *He pauses to look at the covered canvas. He is tempted to take a look.*
>
> **Shona** (*from off*) Dan, after dinner!
>
> **Dan** Nowhere near it, my sweet . . .
>
> *He goes back to the meal.*

Edward It's, ah, it's ah, it's less about sex than you'd think, actually.

Maria   Oh. What a shame.

Edward   It's about the connection between the
visual imagination and . . . well, *thought*, full stop.
That's the interesting question, whether our
language is more about sound or visualisation.

Maria   Mmm.

Edward   Have you ever noticed that if you
visualise a horizon, and then tilt your head from side
to side, the horizon stays level. I say 'level' of course,
but relative to what if it's entirely imaginary –?
Sorry, am I being really insensitive?

Maria   Not at all. No, I thought what you were
saying was very interesting. I can understand it.

Maria *closes her eyes and tips her head, to test what*
Edward *is saying.*

Edward   Ah, you're humouring me.

Maria   Not at all.

Edward   Mmm.

Maria   You're interested in ideas. That's good.

Edward   Well, I've no idea what point I just
made, so . . .

Maria   No, it is good. And I'm guessing you're
quite a big film fan, aren't you?

Edward   Well, it's funny, actually, I've been *reading*
a lot more since doing this job. What? What are you
thinking about?

Maria   I'm thinking about what you were saying.
Visualisation.

Edward   Yes.

Maria   Like . . . fantasising?

Edward   Well –

Maria I'm . . . visualising right now. Sort of.
What do you think I'm thinking?

Edward Ah, I can't possibly imagine.

Maria Try. Go on, guess.

Edward Mm. Ah . . .

Maria What would you like me to be visualising?

Even more awkward moment . . .

> **Shona** *comes in to retrieve her phone, visibly trying to
> control her temper.*
>
> **Shona** (*to off*)   No, it wasn't mine – I must have
> imagined it.

Maria Edward? What are you thinking? Edward?

> **Shona** *goes back out.*

Edward Um . . . I'm thinking . . . Somebody
probably needs to talk to him.

Maria Him? Who?

Edward Greg. Somebody should talk to him.

Maria Greg. It's OK, I'll talk to him tomorrow.

Edward I could have a word with his mother –

Maria She won't be around.

Edward She won't?

Maria Yes.

Edward Does he have problems at home?

Maria Look, Edward . . . The evening got off to
a bad start. Can we just forget about it happening?
Just pretend you didn't see what you did when you
walked in.

Edward A bit easier said than done.

Maria Edward, I just want to leave it. Can we?
This hasn't been much of a date so far – nobody's

fault but – Can we let it pass just for the time being? Please?

Edward Uh . . . Sure. Not a problem. Already forgotten. What were we talking about again?

Maria Thank you.

Edward No problem. Focus on our . . . date.

Very awkward pause.

Maria You still there?

Edward Yes, of course.

Maria Because, if you're not going to say anything to me, you might as well not be there really.

Edward Yes, sorry, yes.

Beat.

It's, er, lovely outside, great – no, mentioned that already . . .

Maria No, it's OK –

Edward Sorry, er, conversation, not always –

Maria No, it's fine –

Edward Sit and talk all day for a living, and not sure what to say myself.

Maria It's not a problem, Edward. You really could say anything. You have a lovely voice. I could easily fancy somebody with a voice like yours.

Edward Would you like to . . . Would you like to . . . touch my face?

Maria Touch your face?

Edward Yes.

Beat.

Maria Touch your face?

Edward If you want to.

Maria *thinks about this, she puts her hand up to touch*
Edward's *face. Then prods and pokes it a couple of times.*

Maria OK, touched that now.

Beat.

What would you like me to touch next?

Edward I'm sorry, I . . . I thought you should put
a face to the voice.

Maria No, I'm sorry. I was . . . Let me try again.

*She leans in and kisses slowly across his face, ending on the
lips. He returns the kiss for a second then pulls away,
standing up.*

Maria Edward?

Edward I thought . . . with your hand . . . Ah . . .
It's getting late.

Maria Is it?

Edward Er, yes.

Maria Oh, yes, I suppose so. I could certainly . . .
handle an early night. Time for bed.

Beat.

Edward Mmm. But he might come back.

Maria He won't.

Edward We can't be sure.

Maria I don't think he will.

Edward It's a possibility.

Maria I doubt it.

Edward Yes, but we can't be certain. Maybe
I should stay.

Beat.

Maria   Well, yes, I suppose there is a chance he might.

Edward   Yes, I probably should stay the night, just in case. I mean he won't, I imagine, but . . .

Maria   No, I would like that. I would really like that.

Edward   Well . . . it's a good job this couch is comfy. Do you have any blankets?

Maria (*nothing*)   Yes. Cupboard in the hall.

Edward   I'll get them.

Edward *leaves to retrieve the blankets.*

Maria   No, it's OK, I can . . .

Edward (*coming back*)   Here we go.

Maria   OK.

Beat.

You mean sleeping now?

Edward   I thought . . . you wanted an early night?

Maria   An early night? Oh . . . well . . . er . . . Time for bed, yes. OK, well . . . anything else you might need?

Edward   No, I'm fine.

Maria *gets up.*

Maria   OK, well, I'll be upstairs if . . . Um, yeah.

Edward   Great.

Maria   Edward?

Edward   Yes?

Maria   Do I get a . . . goodnight . . . hug?

Edward   Of course.

Edward *hugs* **Maria**.

Goodnight. Sleep tight.

Maria   Mm, yeah. I mean, yes, goodnight,
Edward.

She leaves. **Edward** *sits. And thinks.*

— *Time passes.* —

Edward *is asleep on the sofa.*

> **Shona** *storms in with* **Dan**.
>
> **Shona**   Just sit in here while I help wash up.
>
> **Dan**   I can help wash up.
>
> **Shona**   No, just sit in here. Please.
>
> **Dan**   Fine. Whatever you want.
>
> **Shona**   That wasn't funny.
>
> **Dan**   You usually find it funny.
>
> **Shona**   It wasn't. It did not taste a 'bit soapy'.
> It was fine. It was very good, in fact.
>
> **Dan**   I thought it tasted a bit soapy.
>
> **Shona**   It was a fuck of a lot better than anything
> you've ever come up with.
>
> **Dan**   Mmm.
>
> **Shona**   It's funny when it's with your boss in some
> stupid restaurant, but not here. Even then it's
> borderline.
>
> **Dan**   Sorry. But it did taste a bit soapy to me.
>
> **Shona**   Dan, you don't know what you're talking
> about. Cooking means taking dinner out of the
> microwave to stir it once before putting it back in.
>
> **Dan**   I think I have as valid an opinion as any
> other dinner guest.

Shona (*nothing*)

Beat.

Dan   OK. I'm sorry, I was being stupid. I don't know why. I'll go in and apologise to Gaetano if you want.

Shona   No – just . . . stay here, look at these.

She picks up the books and portfolios.

Dan   What are these?

Shona   His work. Just stay out of trouble while we wash up.

She leaves. **Dan** *flicks idly through some of the portfolios, not looking properly at them, until one catches his eye and he begins to flick through them more carefully.*

Edward *stirs.*

Dan   Shona? Shona?

Shona *returns with a glass of wine in her hand.*

Shona   What?

Dan   Have you seen these?

Shona   Seen what?

Dan   These pictures.

Shona   They're pretty good, aren't they?

Dan   These ones. He's not messing about, is he? These are . . . porn. He's just painting pornography.

Shona   At least he's a brushes-and-palette man. That's more your thing, isn't it?

Dan   But look, it is pornography.

Shona   No, it isn't.

Dan   I mean, look at this.

Shona *looks.*

Shona What?

Dan Look . . . she's . . . shaved, look.

Shona No she's just very blonde.

Dan Yeah, but look, right in the middle of the painting. Look how red he's made her . . .

Shona Her what?

Dan Her, look . . .

Shona What? Vulva? *Labia majorae?*

Dan Labby-what?

Shona Cunt lips.

Dan Shona! Jesus . . .

Shona What? Cunt lips?

Dan Shona – Look, you can't complain about me being rude, if you're going to – at least, I'm not sat at the dinner table shouting . . .

Shona Cunt lips? No, you were being rude, I'm just saying what I see.

Dan Keep your voice down, at least.

Shona Keep my voice down? He doesn't give a shit, Dan.

Beat.

Why? Do you have a problem with it, Dan?

Dan Problem with what?

Shona With these pictures.

Dan No.

Shona Yes, you do.

Dan No, of course not.

Shona   Yes, you do. Prudey Dan.

Dan   Yeah, leave it.

Shona   Prudey Dan, blushes at the nudey ladies. Funny feeling in Danny's tummy.

Dan   Yeah, very funny.

Shona   Nothing much more explicit than your average wank-mag.

Dan   I don't know, it's been a while since I had recourse to your average wank-mag.

Shona   Sorry, men's lifestyle magazines –

Dan   They're not wank-mags.

Shona   Whatever you say.

Dan   I have no problem with the female form. Quite the opposite.

Shona   Oh yeah, I bet. Gawking with all the others at the strip club.

Dan   What?

Shona   This place next door – have you really never been there?

Dan   No. I would have known where I was going then, wouldn't I?

Shona   But you have been to one on a 'works outing', haven't you?

Dan   Once or twice. You know I've had to.

Shona   And I bet you weren't shocked then, were you?

Beat.

Dan   Hang on. Are you trying to tell me something?

Shona   What?

Dan   Is a lot of his stuff like . . . this?

Shona   I don't know.

Dan   Is yours . . . like this stuff?

Beat.

Shona   I don't know.

Dan   Come on, really.

Shona   I really don't know. I haven't seen it.
That's the whole point of an unveiling, Dan.

Dan   You must have some idea.

Shona   No, I haven't seen it.

Dan   Not at all?

Shona   No. I have no idea at all. Those ones were
done a long time ago.

Dan   OK.

Shona   It wouldn't bother you if it was, though,
would it?

Beat.

It's just a body. My body. You've taken photographs
of me before.

Dan   Yes, I have. It's not as if I send them in to
Readers' Wives though . . . but, yes I have. No. No.
Of course, it wouldn't bother me. I think it would
be rather great, actually.

Shona   Yeah?

Dan   Yes.

Shona   Not that it is like that. Necessarily.

Dan   Of course.

Shona   I haven't seen it.

Dan   Absolutely.

Shona   Mmm . . . OK.

Dan   I adore your body, so . . .

Shona   Which bits?

Dan   Which bits?

Shona   Yeah.

Dan   I love your . . .

Shona   Yeah?

Dan   Your . . . fabulous breasts.

Shona   They are, aren't they? And?

She hints at her crotch.

Dan   Your arse. You have a fantastic arse.

Shona   And? Go on.

Dan   And . . .?

Shona   You know. Go on, say it. Come on . . . begins with a 'c'. Go on, say it!

Dan   Shona –

Shona   Go on, say it, say it with love, you know you want to.

Dan   Cunt lips.

Shona   Can't hear you.

Dan   All right, cunt lips! Cunt lips, cunt lips, cunt lips!

Gaetano *has come in behind* **Dan**.

Gaetano   Er . . . another glass of wine, anybody?

Beat.

Shona   No, I'm OK, thanks.

Quietly, **Greg** *has come into the room. He studies* **Edward**, *considering what he will do. He is carrying a hammer.*

Dan   Er, yeah. Maybe in a moment.

Gaetano   Fine. OK. Don't think we can wait any longer. Are we ready to see this?

Shona   Very.

Dan   Yes. Fit to burst.

Gaetano *sets about pulling the painting forward so he can whip off the covering sheet in one go.*

Gaetano   Now, Dan, maybe you can give me a hand with the other side of the sheet, and we'll whip it off in three.

Dan   Sure.

Gaetano   Ready? One . . . two . . . three!

The painting is unveiled. Long pause.

Gaetano   So . . . what do we think? Shona?

Shona   Yeah, it's very . . . yeah. Dan, what do you think?

Dan *punches* **Gaetano** *in the face. He falls to the floor.* **Dan** *gives him one hefty kick in the stomach.* **Shona** *pulls* **Dan** *back, thumping him several times in the process.*

Shona   Dan! What the fuck are you doing? Stop it!

Dan   You're a pervert! You're a dirty old man!

Shona *hits* **Dan** *in the arm as hard as she can.*

Dan   Ow!

Shona   I mean it. Stop it.

She goes to **Gaetano** *and helps him up.*

What the fuck did you do that for, Dan? You're a fucking caveman. (*To* **Gaetano**.) Are you OK?

Gaetano   Oh . . . I think so.

Shona   Picked on any other pensioners recently, Dan?

Gaetano   I'm not that old. He caught me off guard.

Dan   Shona, look what he's done!

Shona   Are you sure you're OK?

Gaetano   Yes, I'm fine, just let me get up.

He tries to get up, but needs **Shona***'s help.*

I just need to . . . sit down next door for a moment.

Shona   OK, let's get you –

Gaetano   No, I'm fine, thank you.

Shona   It's OK –

Gaetano   No! I can manage myself, thank you.

Gaetano *leaves, very shaken.*

Greg *kneels by* **Edward***'s head.*

Greg   Hey.

Dan   OK, I know I lost it, but –

Shona   You stupid prick. You stupid, stupid fucker. What was that for?

Dan   I know that was out of order –

Shona   Out of order?

Dan   Shona, look at this!

Shona   Look at what?

Dan   This . . . this!

Shona   What? Me? What's wrong with it?

Dan   Look at it. Look what he's done with your portrait. You didn't know he was going to do that, did you?

Shona   No.

Beat.

Well, I did pose like that, so I had an idea.

Dan   You posed like that?

Shona   Yeah.

Dan   I thought . . . Great. That's fucking great.

Shona   I didn't know what it would look like.

Dan   I thought you were winding me up. You lied to me.

Shona   No, I didn't.

Dan   The yoga? The posing?

Shona   Never said how I posed.

Dan   What else don't I know?

Shona   Dan, you just punched out a man in his sixties, which is more important here? What if he calls the police? What if he presses charges? Are you thinking about this? You fucking idiot! I'm going to see if he's OK, OK?

She leaves **Dan** *to fume.*

Greg   Hey. Hey, wake up. Hey, you.

Greg *prods* **Edward**. *He stirs, sees* **Greg** *and sits bolt upright in panic.*

Edward   Shit! How the hell did you get in here?

Greg   Shh.

Edward   Get out! Go on, piss off or I'll call the police.

Greg   Shh.

Edward   I don't want any trouble. I don't want to call the police if I don't have to. If you leave now . . .

Greg (*nothing*)

Edward   I . . . You can take my wallet if you want. And my phone, too.

Greg (*nothing*)

Edward   Look, I don't know what you think
you're going to do –

Greg   How do you know her?

Edward   What?

Greg   How do you know her?

Edward   She's a friend.

Greg   Friend how?

Edward   Maria? Er, through work. But it's not
really any –

Greg   Why are you here?

Edward   She invited me here. Look, you tell me
what you're doing here, what do you want?

Greg (*nothing*)

Edward   How did you get in here anyway?

Greg   Are you going to hurt her?

Edward   Hurt her? How would I hurt her?

Greg   Are you going to hurt her?

Edward   I don't –

Greg   Are. You. Going. To hurt. Her?

Edward   I would do nothing to hurt her. Ever.
Greg? It is Greg, isn't it?

Greg *stands suddenly.*

Greg   You don't know my name.

Edward   Look, Greg –

Greg   You don't know my name.

Rest.

Edward   OK, fine. Look, I am just a friend that
Maria invited over to dinner. Nothing more. I have
no intentions to . . . hurt her in any sense. I'm just
staying overnight, on the couch, because, ah, it was
late for me to get back, and in the morning, I'll be
gone.

Greg (*nothing*)

Edward   And I haven't told her what you were
doing.

Greg   I wasn't doing anything.

Edward   I did see you –

Greg   You didn't see me. There was nothing to
see.

Edward   Greg –

Greg   You didn't see me!

Maria *has come in, and she intervenes.*

Maria   Greg! Leave him alone. Edward, are you
OK?

Edward   Fine.

Maria   Greg, wait for me by the front door.

Greg *does not move.*

Maria   Greg!

Greg *leaves. Before he goes, he mouths to* **Edward**,
'I will fucking kill you.'

Maria   Are you OK, Edward?

Edward   Yes, I think so, but –

Maria   I won't be a moment.

She leaves to talk to **Greg**.

Shona *comes back in to grab some ice from the ice bucket
for a pack.*

Shona   Well, that was fucking clever.

Edward   What? Wait, where are you going?

Dan   Why did you think we didn't need to discuss this?

Shona   It was nothing to do with you.

Dan   Nothing to do with me.

Shona   It was my choice. It was my thing. It didn't involve you.

Dan   Didn't involve me, right. But you were planning to hang it above my fireplace, yeah? Where everyone can see it?

Shona   No, you didn't understand –

Dan   What are people going to say when they see this?

Shona   Nice tits?

She storms back out.

Dan   Shona!

Maria *comes back in.*

Edward   Maria, are you OK?

Maria   I'm fine. How are you?

Edward   Oh Christ. Bloody hell. My heart is going to jump out of my chest.

Maria   Are you sure you're OK?

Edward   Yes. Well, no, but . . . Oh, Christ. What did you say to him?

Maria   It's all fine. I've sorted it out. A misunderstanding.

Edward   Misunderstanding? Bloody hell. How the hell did he get in here?

Maria   He has a key.

Edward   He has a key? Why does he have a key?

Maria   So he can get in to do all the repairs he does for me.

Edward   What is he going to repair at this time of night? You have to call the police.

Maria   He wasn't going to hurt anybody.

Edward   Hurt anybody?

Maria   He wouldn't have done that.

Edward   No, Maria, he was carrying a –

Maria   Just trust me on this, please, Edward. How about you just trust that I know him? He wouldn't have hurt you or anybody else. There's no need to call the police. He's not done anything.

Edward   Well, yes, they certainly can't get him for breaking and entering if he has a front-door key. He can just wander in and out of here at will?

Maria   Yes. I trust him. He's not going to steal anything.

Edward   Steal anything?

Maria   I wouldn't let him have a key otherwise.

Beat.

Edward   So you know he didn't steal anything?

Maria   Yes.

Edward   You know what he was actually doing?

Maria   Mm, yes.

Edward   What do you think he was actually doing?

Maria   Edward, I know! I could fucking hear him! I know what wanking sounds like. Do you seriously think I don't?

Beat.

Edward Well . . . did you tell him to stop?

> **Shona** *comes back in.*
>
> **Dan** Shona, I fucked up, I am so, so sorry. I've been trying really hard to do the right thing . . .

Maria Obviously not, no.

> **Dan** I mean . . .

Edward Has he . . . Has he done that before?

> **Shona** He's not calling the police, but he wants you to leave now.
>
> **Dan** He wants us to leave. Well, yeah, let's get out of here.
>
> **Shona** *You.*
>
> **Dan** Me.

— Rest. —

Edward Have you been sleeping with him?

> **Dan** (*simultaneously*) Have you been fucking him, then?
>
> **Shona** You what?

Maria Having sex with him?

> **Dan** Is that it? You're fucking him?

Maria Oh, he'd run a mile if I tried.

> **Shona** Right. He's twice my age. He's older than my dad.
>
> **Dan** Is that a yes?
>
> **Shona** Fuck off.

Edward But you enjoy him doing that?

> **Dan** No, really, is that a yes? Yes or no?

Shona Do I have to answer that? Are you expecting me to answer that?

Maria I don't know.

Dan You could say nothing at all if you want.

Shona I shouldn't have to.

Edward Do you want him to . . . have sex with you?

Maria Oh, Edward, he's not about to fuck the nice blind lady. He's far too *honourable* for that.

Edward But masturb – *wanking* in front of her is OK, though?

Maria Not that that's something I particularly want to happen either. It's not what I'm looking for.

Dan *Is* that a no?

Shona No! No, you stupid fuckwit, no!

— *Beat.* —

Edward But you do let him do that?

Dan (*simultaneously*) But you did lie about this?

— *Rest.* —

Maria I guess I have done, yes . . .

Shona I didn't *lie*. I kept something for myself. Can you see the difference?

Dan Yourself and your work colleagues.

Shona Oh, it's just a fucking painting, Dan.

Dan Oh, would Gae-fucking-whatever agree with you on that, then?

Maria He did it once . . .

Shona Hundreds of people have done it. Hundreds of people are freezing their fucking arses off lying around right now.

Dan   And how many of them are fucking the artist as well?

Shona   That doesn't mean I am!

Maria   And I guess I let him, yes. And then I let him do it again.

Dan   I'll buy it off him.

Maria   A . . . few times.

Dan   Yeah, I'll buy it off him.

Shona   And do what?

Dan   What?

Shona   And do what with it?

Maria   If I knew why I let him do it, then I probably wouldn't let him do it.

Shona   And do what? Paint a dress on me?

Dan   Shona.

Shona   Or how about a veil, head-to-toe?

Dan   Shona, you have the most beautiful face of any woman I have ever known –

Shona   Cut my head off my fucking body, then, Dan! Crime of passion, might get away with it.

Dan   Shona, do you even *want* to live together?

Beat.

Shona   What does that have to do with anything?

Dan   Where do you want to hang this, then?

Shona   I won't hang it anywhere, it doesn't belong to –

Dan   Pride of place, above the mantelpiece? Yeah? So Mum and Dad come over for coffee, with you lounging around them naked? Or I can bring the lads in after football and we can chat about your tits? Or maybe when the boss comes over for dinner, I can show him my wife's *cunt*.

Beat.

Shona   *Wife's* cunt?

Maria   Edward?

Dan   Girlfriend's – What-fucking-ever!

— Rest. —

Edward   Do you want me to leave?

Dan (*simultaneously*)   Do *you* want me to leave?

Maria   Leave?

Edward   I mean – maybe I should go.

Maria   No.

Shona   Er, yes, I think Gaetano would be much happier if you did, yeah.

Dan   Do *you* want me to go?

Rest.

Edward   Probably best if I did . . . go.

Shona   No. Not yet. You still haven't answered my question.

Dan   What question?

Shona   What do you think?

Dan   Think of what?

She nods at the painting.

Shona   What do you think?

— Nobody says anything. —

Maria   Edward?

Dan   Ah, Shona, I –

Shona   What?

— Nobody says anything. A long moment. —

| Say something.

— Nobody says anything. —

| Come on, say something!

— Nobody says anything. —

Edward   I'm sorry.

He leaves.

Shona   Right. So the fat woman in the airport gets a mention, but now you're tongue-tied.

Dan   Fuck this. I'm gone.

Shona   No, hang on – Dan, it's just . . . You've stopped looking at me the way you used to. And that's so *soon*.

Dan   OK. I better had go.

Shona   Dan.

Dan   I'll . . . we'll talk . . .

He leaves.

Shona   Dan. Wait.

But she lets him go.

Maria *is sat on the sofa.*

Shona *sits on the sofa.* **Gaetano** *comes back in.*

Shona   He's gone.

Gaetano   Yes, I heard him. I'm sorry this caused so much trouble.

Shona   It was all him, don't you worry. Stupid prick.

Gaetano   You weren't to know he'd do that.

Beat.

Shona   No.

Gaetano   He loves you, doesn't he?

Shona   Love? He hit you because he loves me?
Yeah, right.

Rest.

I'm not sure I've ever been in love.

Gaetano (*nothing*)

Shona   It can't just be these fucking stupid
compromises. Can it? Everyone tells it like it's
fireworks and meteor showers. Well, I've never seen
them.

Rest.

How's your face?

Gaetano   It'll live. It will make me look more
interesting. It's a shame I'm not exhibiting any time
soon . . .

Shona   I'm sorry about Dan. I never thought he'd
react like that. I completely misjudged him. I made
a complete misjudgement.

Gaetano   Had you not thought much about how
he'd react, then?

Beat.

Shona   What's that supposed to mean?

Gaetano   Well, I'd just observed – It's none of my
business.

Shona   What?

Gaetano   Weren't you trying to get some kind of
reaction from him?

Shona   Not that.

Gaetano   What did you expect to happen, then?
Seriously?

Shona   OK, right, and you didn't ask me if I'd model for you just because you wanted to see my tits, then?

Beat.

Gaetano   You're right, I'm sorry. It is none of my business. Dan wasn't quite . . . wasn't quite what *I* was expecting, I suppose.

Beat.

Shona   No, I'm actually asking you that.

Gaetano   Asking me . . .?

Shona   Did you ask me to pose for you because you wanted to see me naked?

Beat.

Gaetano   Right. Well, of course, yes. I mean, I wanted to paint you. I didn't want to paint your clothes, what you were wearing.

Shona   I'm only me when I'm naked?

Beat.

Did you fancy me?

Gaetano   You're a bit young for me.

Shona   Is that a yes? This afternoon . . . did you touch the painting at all? Or did you just look?

Gaetano   I could have taken photographs if that was all I wanted.

Shona   I thought you couldn't paint from photos?

Gaetano   I don't think you can. I think they're very different. A photo . . . is nothing. It's just an eye. It's a moment caught like a butterfly. A painting is . . . a physical record. Of strokes. Of caresses . . .

Shona   Have you ever been to the club next door?

Gaetano   You've not asked me this before.

Shona   I wasn't curious before. Have you? Why couldn't one of the girls at the bar have posed for you?

Gaetano   They're usually busy at night.

Shona   You could pay them?

Gaetano   Not as much as they get there.

Shona   What if one offered a discount?

Gaetano   I don't think that's likely.

Shona   But what if?

Gaetano   They're not . . . right.

Shona   How?

Gaetano   There's nothing . . . there to paint.

Shona   Nothing there?

Gaetano   Yes.

Shona   Nothing to look at?

Gaetano   No, I mean –

Shona   Or: you can look but you can't touch?

Gaetano   Oh, all right, fuck it! Yes, I fancied you. I fancy you, yes, I think of you naked and writhing when I'm pulling myself off, is that what you want to know?

Beat.

Is that what you wanted to hear? I can't imagine it's that much of a surprise in the grand scheme of things. I am flesh and blood.

Beat.

Shona   No.

Gaetano   No? I certainly don't paint for the money, I'd have thought that was obvious.

Beat.

Come on, that is exactly what you've been wanting to hear, isn't it?

Shona (*nothing*)

Gaetano   Oh, don't look so fucking scandalised – how about we cut out the pretence altogether, you pop your clothes off on the chair, I'll just sit here and get my dick out. And if you get off on me getting off you can have a bit of a fiddle yourself.

Shona   OK, sorry I asked.

Gaetano   Well, now you know. And I imagine the pleasure's in knowing, isn't it?

Beat.

I mean – Of course it is . . . Don't be sorry. There's nothing wrong with that, it's perfectly human activity. There's nothing wrong with that at all.

Beat.

Shona   Do you really . . .?

Gaetano   What shall we do about this painting, then? Shall I arrange to have it delivered?

Shona   Delivered? No, I can't afford it.

Gaetano   Oh, it won't cost much. My nephew can bring it round.

Shona   No, I mean the painting itself. I can't possibly afford it.

Gaetano   It won't be worth that much. It will be worth more to you than it will be to me. Just look after it, that's all I ask.

Shona   I can't just take it.

Gaetano   Why not? Evidently, I'll only sit in front of it and toss myself off into oblivion. And nobody deserves to stumble onto that particular death scene.

Beat.

My jaw's going to ache every time I look at it. It's yours. It really is. Please take it.

She thinks.

Shona   I will take it. Thank you.

Gaetano   Great.

Shona   I better go and talk to Dan.

Gaetano   Yes. You better had.

She gathers her stuff to leave.

Shona   OK. Thank you. Goodnight.

Gaetano   Yes. Take care. And it was a pleasure working with you. For many reasons. All at once.

Beat.

Shona   Yes, likewise. Bye.

She leaves.

Maria *is sitting alone.*

Gaetano   Nothing wrong with it at all . . .

He leaves the studio. The lights in the studio dim.

Edward *comes back in.*

Edward   It's quite dark outside now.

Maria   Edward?

Edward   I don't know really where I'm going. I was going to ring for a taxi, but I've not got a signal. I don't know any taxi numbers either, so . . .

Maria   I think there are some by the phone.

Rest.

Edward   Did you leave the front door open deliberately?

Maria   What do you mean?

Edward   When I came in tonight. Had you left it open deliberately so I'd walk in on . . . what I walked in on?

Maria   No. I don't think so. It was Greg that left it open behind him probably.

Edward   But you didn't check that it was closed? Did you know I was about to turn up?

Maria   You were earlier than – Yes. I don't know, maybe I was expecting you. I don't know what I was doing.

Beat.

Edward   So you knew I was lying?

Maria   Yes.

Edward   And you let me carry on?

Maria   Yes, I guess I did.

Beat.

Edward   What was I supposed to do? I'd just walked in the bloody door! What if I had called the police? I had no chance! Was it some kind of test?

Maria   No.

Edward   It wasn't fair. How was I meant to react?

Maria   You weren't meant to –

Edward   Why on earth did you invite me here in the first place?

Maria   I hope, for the same reason that you accepted the invitation.

Edward   Yes, of course. I mean, I wanted to come, but – I wasn't expecting any of this.

Maria   What were you expecting to happen?

Rest.

Are you going to leave? I understand if you want to go.

Edward   Not yet. No.

Maria   Good, I want you to stay. I know it's all gone a bit . . . I mean, it's all gone a bit . . . I want you to stay.

She moves closer to him. She puts a hand out to his face. She moves to kiss him, he returns the kiss but then breaks.

Edward   No . . . I . . . Sorry. No.

Maria   What is it? It's OK.

Edward   No, I don't feel . . .

Maria   What?

Edward   I'm . . . I shouldn't be . . .

Maria   What? Edward? What is it?

Rest.

Edward, do you like women?

Edward   Um, yes, no, I . . .

Maria   Do you like me?

Edward   Yes, I . . .

Maria   Are you a virgin?

Edward (*nothing*)

Maria   Edward. Are you a –

Edward   No.

No, it's just that, I'm . . . I shouldn't be . . . I don't know . . . taking advantage, I don't know.

Maria   Taking advantage? Of what?

Edward   I mean . . . I . . .

Edward *moves to get up, but* **Maria** *holds him.*

Maria   No, what? Tell me. Go on, what?

Edward I didn't mean that. It's just – I don't have the – words for this. I can't . . .

Maria Can you try? Go on, tell me.

Edward It doesn't feel like it's meant to. It's not gone how it's meant to.

Maria How is it meant to go?

Beat.

Edward I don't know.

Maria So, how do you know how it's meant to feel?

Edward It just . . . isn't how I imagined it.

Maria You've imagined this?

Edward I . . .

Maria You've fantasised about this?

Edward (*nothing*)

Maria Have you thought about me while wanking?

Edward No . . . I . . .

Maria Have you thought about this situation while wanking?

Edward (*nothing*)

Maria And is it better or worse than how you imagined it?

Maria *stands up, and takes off her robe so she stands naked.*

Look at me. What do I look like?

Edward Maria. You don't have to –

Maria What? Don't have to do what?

What do I look like?

Edward Maria –

Maria What do I look like?

Edward You're . . . You're beautiful.

Maria No, what do I look like? My body, what does it look like?

Edward I don't know what to −

Maria My mouth, what does it look like?

Edward It's . . . pretty. It's −

Maria No. Exactly. Colour. Shape.

Edward *describes her mouth.*

Maria And my . . . arms?

Edward *describes exactly her arms.*

Maria And my neck? And my shoulders?

Edward *describes exactly her neck and her shoulders.*

Maria And my breasts?

Edward *describes exactly her breasts.*

Maria Now. Stand up.

Maria *sits.* **Edward** *stands.*

Maria Undress. Undress.

Edward *takes off his clothes.*

Maria Are you looking at me?

Edward Yes.

Maria Stand in front of me.

Are you hard?

Are you hard?

Edward Yes.

Maria Are you touching it?

Touch it. Bring yourself off.

Are you doing it?

Edward *begins to masturbate, standing in front of* **Maria**.

Maria   Edward?

Edward   Yes. Yes.

Maria   OK. Now kiss me.

Edward *sits next to* **Maria**. *They kiss. They kiss more and they lie down together on the sofa.*

Scene Three

Monday lunchtime. A recording booth, cramped and confined. Desk with a microphone and a computer screen. And a woman sitting at the desk, staring out into space. She snaps out of it and starts recording again, pausing and pressing a key between each piece of recording to skip between the film dialogue she is listening to on headphones.

Shona   Zack, still in his spotless white navy officer uniform, marches into the mill where everyone is hard at work.

She presses a key.

Surprised to see him, the mill workers follow him to see where he is going.

She presses a key.

Zack marches up behind Paula. He kisses her on the neck, and she turns around.

She presses a key.

They kiss as Lynette looks on astonished.

She presses a key.

Zack and Paula embrace. He sweeps her up into his arms, and her workmates stand by applauding, as Zack carries Paula all the way out of the factory.

Beat.

And straight into a small one-bedroom trailer, where she is condemned to pop out little naval officer babies for the rest of her life, and suffer boring, routine sex with a slimy, vain bastard who smells of piss.

Beat. **Shona** *sighs. She re-records.*

He sweeps her up into his arms, and her workmates stand by applauding, as Zack carries Paula all the way out of the factory.

Rest. **Shona** *takes off the headphones.* **Edward** *is at the door behind her. A red light flashes above* **Shona** *and she lets* **Edward** *in. He has a mobile on him.*

Shona   Hi, Edward, how are you?

Edward   Very well, thank you. Er, your phone kept ringing.

Shona   Sorry, should have switched it off.

Edward   Hope you don't mind, it was ringing a lot, so I answered it. He says it's quite urgent.

Shona *takes the phone. She looks at the caller ID, and switches the phone off. She turns back to face the video screen.*

Edward   Oh.

Shona   How was your weekend?

Edward   Ah. It was great. Eventful. Great. Sorry, should I have ignored it (*ie, the phone*)?

Shona   No, it's fine. How did the date go?

Beat.

Edward   It's funny, but I –

Shona   Do you believe in love at first sight, Edward?

Edward   Love?

Shona   Yeah.

Edward   Er . . . No, it's a bit of a cliché, isn't it?

Shona   Yes. Absolutely.

Beat.

It's absolute bollocks.

You know I hadn't seen Dan for years when we got together? I just bumped into him in a bar?

Edward   Yes. You had mentioned it once or twice . . .

Shona   Within twenty-four hours, we'd seen everything. We'd made love together, bathed together, slept together. He'd seen my body. I'd seen his. From every angle.

Which bit are you meant to fall in love with?

Beat.

Edward   Er . . . Shona, did something happen with you and Dan? Is he trying to ring you?

Shona   Oh no, that was Gaetano.

Edward   Gaetano?

Shona   The artist.

Edward   Oh yes, the artist.

Shona   Did I tell you he's painted a portrait of me?

Edward   A few times –

Shona   Well . . . he's painted a portrait of me. We saw it on Friday night.

Edward   Great. How was it? Or . . . is that why you're not talking to him?

Shona   No, it was . . . great. I just think he won't be very pleased when I tell him I want to I cut his painting in half.

Edward   Cut it in half?

Shona   Oh no, it still works like that. I get two for the price of one. One for the bedroom, one for the downstairs loo.

Beat.

Edward   So, how was it? Er, them? How are . . . they?

Shona   No, it was OK.

Edward   Nothing too abstract, then?

Shona   No . . . it looked . . . pretty accurate.

Edward   You don't seem too enthusiastic about it?

Shona   No. It was . . . great.

Beat.

Edward   You didn't want to make more of a show of it, then?

Shona *shrugs.*

Edward   Fair enough. Don't want to go shoving it in people's faces, I suppose.

Rest.

Shona   I can't move in with Dan.

I don't think it's going to last. Everybody can see that. I'm just catching up, aren't I?

Beat.

Edward   I don't know.

Shona   I don't have to say it out loud just yet, though, do I?

Beat.

There's no real hurry.

Beat.

Sorry, you were telling me about your weekend?

Edward   Oh, yes. Er . . . well −

Shona   I tease you too much, Edward, don't I?

Edward (*nothing*)

Shona   I'm not going to tease you as much any more. I'd better get on with this. Almost finished.

She puts on the headphones and gets back to watching the video image. She is not listening to **Edward**.

Edward   Well . . . since you did ask . . . It went very well.

I ended up staying with Maria out in the countryside for the whole weekend. And I very much enjoyed it. And she and I went out to the pub this one night. And we walked back in the dark. And it was wonderful, an incredibly clear night after a cloudless day, the smell of this cleansed air . . . I'd forgotten how good the air *smells*. When it's clean like that. When it's been cooked by the sun during the day, and it cools at night . . .

And the stars! I'd almost forgotten what they looked like. All the light pollution in the city, all that interference, you can't get any idea of them at all.

But out there in the darkness you could see everything.